This book
belongs to:

A DELL TRADE PAPERBACK

Published by
Dell Publishing
a division of
Bantam Doubleday Dell Publishing Group, Inc.
666 Fifth Avenue
New York, New York 10103

ISBN: 0-440-50438-4

Printed in the United States of America
Published simultaneously in Canada

April 1992

10 9 8 7 6 5 4 3 2 1

KPH

YOU CAN'T SELL YOUR BROTHER AT THE GARAGE SALE!

THE KIDS' BOOK OF VALUES

By BETH BRAINARD

and ILLUSTRATED BY SHEILA BEHR

A Dell Trade Paperback

Also by Beth Brainard and Sheila Behr

SOUP SHOULD BE SEEN, NOT HEARD!

The Kids' Etiquette Book

This book is dedicated
with love to my sons,
Nate and Zach.

Beth Brainard

And to my grandchildren,
Nicki, Steven, Michael,
Abby, Jason, David, Allie,
and Kevin.

Mama Behr

This book is about
VALUES

Values are actions and beliefs that <u>all</u> people agree are **good**, like honesty, taking responsibility, and doing your best.

Values are **important** because they help you tell the difference between right and wrong.

To be a **good person**, every kid needs a **good set of values.**

Here are some important values.

Dear Kids,

   This book is written just for you! Read on and we will show you how values help you to be a good person.

Hi!

Your friends,
THE Good Idea Kids

This is what's in the book:

Here we go!

I Like My Freckles

(Respect Yourself)

♪ KIDS' BILLBOARD ♪

Good Idea Kids Top 8 Hits
Will Take You to Self-Respect

1. Know Yourself
2. Take Care of Your Body
3. Look Good (Pride in Appearance)
4. Be Polite
5. Be Honest
6. Have a Sense of Humor
7. Be Positive
8. Do Your Best

TEEN MAGA
Good Idea Kids
Have a Message

TOUR
Good Idea Kids
In NY, Paris

3

Self-respect is an important value. The first step you have to take is to **know yourself**.

Find out who you are by interviewing yourself. Ask questions like:

- What do I like or dislike to do, to play, to see, to eat?
- What are my strong points?
- What could I do better?
- What do my friends like about me?

Keep asking questions until you know **you**.

It's fun!

Now that you're a star, are you going to have those freckles removed?

No, I'm not. I <u>like</u> my freckles. They're part of who I am.

Change the things about yourself that you can - like bad habits.

Accept the things that you can't change - like your freckles.

Remember, kids, NO ONE IS PERFECT.

5

Come on, Parker. It's about time for rehearsal.

I'll be with you in a minute. I've got to get cleaned up first.

Take pride in your **appearance** because if you look good, you feel good about yourself.

Be neat, wear clean clothes, polish your shoes, take care of your skin, teeth, hair, and nails.

Oh— don't forget to stand up straight.

To feel good about yourself, you also need to feel good.
Take care of your body by eating nutritious foods,
exercising regularly, getting enough rest, and bathing
daily. DON'T SMOKE OR TAKE DRUGS.

7

T.J., would you please pass the Ketchup?

Kids, you should always **be polite**. Use good manners and treat others the way you would like them to treat you.

8

Be honest. It's not always easy, but it is important to do what you know is right. When you tell the truth, you will feel good.

9

CONSTRUCTION
PROBLEMS
___
GOOD IDEA KIDS
CONCERT
CANCELED

BOX OFFICE
CLOSED

CANCELED

FREE
CONCERT →

GOOD IDEA
KIDS

LEMONADE
25¢

Your life is what you make it, so be positive.

When the world hands you lemons, make lemonade.

Don't be so serious that you can't have any fun. Have a sense of humor. Be able to laugh at yourself.

11

 My mom's taking us out to eat. Do you want to come, Parker?

 Thank you, but no. I'm having trouble playing that last song, so I'm going to stay here and practice until I get it right.

Your work is a reflection of you, so always make an effort to **do your best.**

13

Heavy!

CHAPTER TWO

It's All in Your Mind

(Use Your Head)

Kids who use their minds have a lot of fun.

Kids who don't are usually bored. They have dull lives.

-Ho Hum.

So, it's a good idea to turn on your brain

oo (it'll work anywhere)

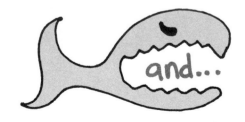

and...

Poor kid.
He's growing
sprouts!

turn off the
T.V. and video games.

Watching or playing a
little is fun, but too
much will turn you into

COUCH POTATOES

and

VIDEO VEGETABLES!

17

Now, tune in your imagination.

Find fun, interesting things to do.

— Wow!

Try new things.

Paint instead of color, learn a new board game, go to an exhibit at your museum or science center, try a new flavor of ice cream.

19

Build up your brain power. The more you know, the more interesting your life will be.

Do your best in school.

Keep learning your whole life.

READ!

BUS STOP

← Ashley has common sense.

Along with facts, you need to **learn common sense**.

Common sense is ordinary good judgment. You learn it from everyday life experiences.

You have to know enough to come in out of the rain!

21

Meet and talk with all
different kinds of people.
You'll be surprised what you learn!

Learn to share your thoughts and ideas with others. Be a good talker and a good listener. (It takes a little practice.)

Talking Steps

- Pick a good time - when you have the listener's attention.
- Look the person in the eye.
- Speak clearly.
- SAY WHAT YOU MEAN — no one can read your mind!
- Be accurate and honest.

Think before you speak.

Listening Steps

- Give the person a chance to talk. Don't interrupt.
- Look the person in the eye.
- Pay attention.
- Ask questions if you don't understand.

23

Be open-minded.

Kids, you need to be willing to listen to and think about new ideas.

Most of the great inventors and doers of the world have been called crazy. But just look at what became of their ideas!

You know, it's said that if a person can come up with an idea, sooner or later, someone will be able to make it real.

Think about it!

25

Brain Power!

CHAPTER THREE

The Big "R"

(Take Responsibility)

29

First, you need to show that you can be trusted.

Earn the trust of others by being honest, loyal, and fair.

Next, learn the difference between right and wrong and do what you know is right.

Third, do the things you are expected to do (like homework and chores) without being told.

Last of all, learn to make good decisions ...

How to Make Good Decisions

1. Get all the facts

2. Look at the reasons for and against (make a list if you'd like)

3. Think about all the possible solutions.

4. Pick the best solution.

5. Do it!

Here are some examples of decisions you may have to make:

- to spend your birthday money or put it in the bank

- to do your homework or watch T.V.

- to go home on time or keep playing with your friends

GREAT THINGS HAPPEN TO RESPONSIBLE KIDS

- Your family and friends respect you.

- You are offered special opportunities — like being a school safety patrol.

Cool!

- You are allowed to do more things because your parents and teachers know you can be trusted.

Hi, Ashley. You're home right on time.

Everyone has responsibilities.

You have responsibilities... as a family member and friend.

- Be loving, kind, and caring.

- Be honest.

- Be loyal.

- Respect the feelings and possessions of others.

- Share.

- Be courteous.

There's the bell.
It's time to go in.

SCHOOL

RING! RING!

... as a student

- Pay attention and participate in class.

- Do your work.

- Be honest.

- Be kind and fair.

- Use good manners.

- Obey school rules.

- DO YOUR BEST.

... as a citizen

- Know how your government works.

- Obey the laws.

- Be loyal to your country.

- Fight injustice.

- Protect the environment.

- Vote (when you're 18!).

37

Can you handle it?

CHAPTER FOUR

You Can't Sell Your Brother at the Garage Sale!

(Get Along with  Your Family)

Treat your family like friends, and your friends like family.

You may be tempted to sell your brother at a garage sale, but don't. Think of him as a <u>person</u> instead of a brother.

My brother is a dog.

41

Get to know each member of your family.

O.K. Mom and Dad, let me get this straight— <u>you two</u> used to stay up late, eat pizza, and listen to rock 'n' roll?

oh-oh!

Parents are people, too!

Show you care.

Good night, Mom. Love you.

Good night, honey. I love you, too.

Be thoughtful, kind, and loving to your family. Give them lots of smiles, hugs, and kisses.

43

Respect everyone's

feelings
privacy
possessions
space.

Knock-Knock

May I come in?

Obey your
family's rules.

Be loyal to your family.

Hey! Don't pick on my little brother!

Stand by them.

Protect them.

Confide in them.

Be honest with them.

45

Learn from them.

Parents and grandparents have had a lot of experiences. The things they know can help you.

(You might even learn something from your big sister!)

My big sister is a real woofer.

Some Family Tips from the Good Idea Kids

- Treat steps (parents, brothers, sisters) the same way you treat the rest of your family.
- Share.
- Don't tease.
- Be nice to your family's friends.
- Don't do or say hateful things.
- Admit when you're wrong and apologize.
- Pick up after yourself!
- Do your share of the household chores.
- Be courteous to family help (like the maid, baby sitter, handyman, etc.).
- Take responsibility for your things.
- Always use good manners.
- Don't eat all the snacks!

47

Sometimes you may feel that your parents love your brother or sister more than they love you. You may feel hurt, angry, envious, and resentful — that's jealousy. What you need to know is that parents love <u>all</u> their children all the time.

Your parents may treat you differently than they treat your brother because you and your brother are two <u>different</u> people.

Fight feelings of jealousy because they only hurt you.

A Note from the Good Idea Kids about Jealousy and Tattling

Don't tattle on brothers or sisters just to make yourself look good. **Do** tell when you know what they're doing is truly wrong, harmful, dangerous, or against the law.

How to Handle Terrible Family Problems

Divorce · Alcohol/Drug Abuse · Physical/Sexual Abuse

Sickness · Mental Illness · Money Problems · Death

I have to tell you something.

- **Don't run away** – it doesn't solve anything. Find help instead.

- **Be strong** – use your mind and your courage to face the problem.

- **Support your family** – try to be understanding and loyal.

- **Find someone to talk to** – someone you trust who will listen and maybe offer some good advice.

49

CHAPTER FIVE

Friends Count

(Be a Good Friend)

T.J., Suzi, Parker, and I would like to share what we've learned about friends.

Read on . . .

53

How to Make Friends

by T.J. Jones

When I want to make a new friend, I just act like myself. I find a kid who likes some of the same things I do. Then, I talk to him for a while. If we get along, I ask him if he'd like to come over sometime.

I like to make friends with all different kinds of kids.

Also, I take my friends just the way they are. No one's perfect—not even me (ha,ha).

My first sleepover with Parker and Matt.

How to Keep Friends

by Ashley Adams

To have friends, you have to be a friend. My mom says "Friendship is a two-way street."

I think the best way to keep friends is to be honest, kind, and caring.

- Respect your friends.

    Share your thoughts and feelings as well as your belongings with them.

Friendship takes some work, but it's worth it!

← When Suzi broke her leg, I took Fifi over for a cheer-up visit.

My Real Friends

by Suzi Sage

There are a lot of kids I know and get along with, and then there are my real friends. My real friends like me just the way I am, and they're my friends <u>all</u> the time. Whenever I need help or someone to talk to, my real friends are there. Sometimes we get mad at each other, but we work out our problems. My real friends are fun to be with. They make me feel good.

My real friends are so cool. I hope you have some real friends, too.

My Summer with The Blades
(The Wrong Crowd)

by Parker Payne

Last summer, I hung around with The Blades. They're a gang that goes to my school. At first, I thought they were really cool, and they really seemed to like me. Things changed. The minute I joined, they wanted me to change the way I dressed. Instead of playing ball or fishing, they hung out around the playground smoking. Their idea of a good time was spray-painting swear words on buildings. They picked on little kids and old people. One time they wanted me to steal a bike. When I said no, they called me "chicken" and "baby." The Blades thought everyone and everything was stupid and boring. Really, The Blades were the stupid, boring ones.

I quit The Blades and found some real friends. I am having a much better time now.

61

What We've Learned about Friendship

by The Good Idea Kids

Friends share your likes and dislikes.

Friends like you just the way you are.

Friends can be trusted.

Friends are fun. They make you feel good.

← Man's best friend.

You gotta have friends.

CHAPTER SIX

Different Doesn't Mean Less

(Fight Prejudice)

People are different.

This means "O.K." in my country.

In Japan, it means "money".

I can't say what it means in Brazil, because I'll be sent to my room!

Each group of people has their own way of doing things.

Americans like medium rare steak. The Chinese like raw monkey brains.

There are no right or wrong meats. There are only <u>different</u> meats.

That's how it is with people, too.

Other ways people are different:

Nationality
Skin Color
Sex
Language
Religion
Clothing
Gestures and Expressions
Mental or Physical Handicaps
Places They Live
Foods They Eat
Jobs They Do
Values (some values are universal,
   but some differ from country to
   country.)

When you meet someone who is different than you, Keep an open mind.

Talk. Find out what you have in common. Learn.

Remember, kids, the world wouldn't be interesting if everyone were exactly the same.

Accept and Respect other ways.

Prejudice Is a Problem

Prejudice is the feeling of disliking people just because they're different.

If you decide you don't
like someone before you
get to know them...

...you could miss out
on a lot of good
friends.

Oui, Oui

I don't like the way you're talking about Ashley. It's <u>wrong</u>. We're not going to play with you.

You can help make the world a nicer place by fighting prejudice.

- Don't make fun of people because they're different.

- Never use ugly racial or ethnic names. Speak up when others do. Tell them you don't like it.

- Don't quietly go along with a group that does prejudice things. Try to get them to change.

Years ago, people from different countries only saw each other on vacations.

Say cheese!

Things have changed.

Technology has made travel quick and easy. Businesses have offices and people all over the world. Lots of people move to other countries to live. (You probably have kids in your school who are different races and nationalities.)

We are now a Global Society and we are all citizens of the world.

GET ALONG!

Dogs of the world, UNITE!

CHAPTER SEVEN

Do a Good Deed

(Get Involved)

By helping others,
you make the world
a better place.

Get involved!

Be doers.

It is a good idea to know what is happening in your community and in the world.

Watch or listen to the news.

Read the newspaper. (You don't have to read it cover to cover, but do make a practice of scanning the headlines then reading stories that interest you.)

Then, you will know where and when help is needed.

On the news, there was a report about homeless people in our town.

Maybe our scout pack could do something to help.

ANIMAL ···· SHELTER ···

WATER

DOG FOOD

Places that help others also need help. Libraries, hospitals, retirement homes, day care centers, parks, animal shelters, even police departments have jobs that can be done by volunteers.

Pick a place that you would like to help, call the volunteer coordinator there, find out what you could do.

A Good Volunteer...

Follows directions
Uses his/her head (THINKS!)
Is responsible
Takes initiative
Doesn't quit until the job is done
Doesn't complain about the job given
Arrives on time to work
Arranges for a substitute if he/she
  cannot work
Never acts "better" than others
Dresses appropriately
Uses good manners
Is always thinking of ways to make
  things better

JOIN A GROUP THAT DOES GOOD THINGS

like scouts, student council, or a church youth group.

LEARN HOW TO WORK IN A GROUP

It is important to know how to get along in a group because a lot more good can be done when people work together.

- Attend meetings regularly.
- Follow the rules and be courteous
- Take part in decisions by voicing your opinion. Vote.
- Once a decision is made about an activity or project, do your best to make it a success.

Think of things you and/or the group you belong to can do to help others.

Do your good deeds quietly.

(Don't brag or do them just for the glory.)

Always lend a helping hand.

Your reward is the good feeling of knowing that you have helped others.

85

Volunteer!

CHAPTER EIGHT

Turn Out the Lights!

(Protect the Environment)

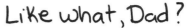

There is too much trash!
Try not to make much more.

Recycle paper, glass, plastic,
and aluminum.

Reuse as many products and
containers as you can.

Refuse to buy products or
services that harm the
environment.

Hold on to your balloon, Kelly.
Loose balloons are harmful
to birds and animals.

Thank you
for the tip,
Ashley.

Be sure to teach your
parents and friends tips
you have learned.

89

Some Tips from the Good Idea Kids on Conserving Energy

Turn out lights you're not using.

Don't run the dishwasher or other "loadable" appliances until they're full.

Keep your house thermostat at 70°, then add or take off clothing to be comfortable.

Buy rechargeable batteries.

Use hot water wisely.

Only open the refrigerator when it is necessary.

Cover pots when heating or boiling water, etc. (Pot bottoms should be the same size as the burner.)

When it is very hot or cold outside, keep blinds and curtains closed.

Do try to walk or ride your bike more and ride in the car less. You will save energy and help keep the air clean.

Do try to avoid using products that use CFCs. CFCs are chemicals that destroy the ozone layer.

CFCs are found in some plastics and foam packing materials. They are also in the coolants used in refrigerators and air conditioners.

Maybe <u>you</u> will invent a replacement for CFCs that isn't harmful!

91

Save the water!

Don't waste it.

Did you know that you can save 5 gallons of water a day by simply turning off the faucet when you brush your teeth?

Find out some other ways you can save water.

Don't be a polluter.

Protect and plant trees wherever you can.

Don't trample, pick, or rip plants when you're outside.

Plant a tree on Earth Day and Arbor Day.

Don't buy products made from endangered species. Ivory, certain furs and reptile skins, tortoise shell, coral and some shells are on the list. Find out before you buy.

Take a Stand

against greedy people
and companies who are
destroying the environment
just to make a buck.

WRITE LETTERS to
government officials
and to the companies!

How to Write Government Officials

President _____
The White House
Washington D.C. 20501
(Dear Mr. President:)

Senator _____
U.S. Senate
Washington D.C. 20510
(Dear Senator _____:)

Representative _____
U.S. House of Representatives
Washington D.C. 20515
(Dear Ms. _____:)

Parker Payne
2114 Linde
Ft+it1

Mr. Douglas Dondrel
YYZ Corporation

Dear Sir,
Shame on
for polluti
lakes

Speak Out!

THINK GREEN

Ush
House
D.C. 20501

Each of us has a responsibility (The big "R" again) to **DO SOMETHING!**

To find out more ways you can help the environment, go to your library or bookstore. There are a lot of good books for kids on the subject.

Please don't wait until it's too late!

CITY PARK

CANDY BAR

TRASH

CANDY   PEANUTS

97

Think green!

CHAPTER NINE

Don't Spend it All in One Place

(Use Your Money Wisely)

Rich, poor, or in the middle, everyone needs to learn how to use their money wisely.

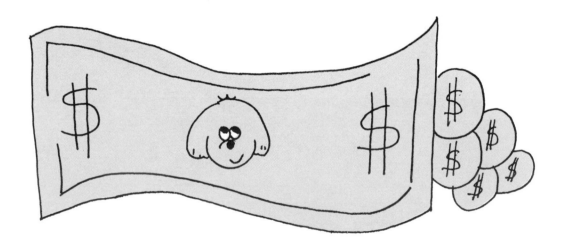

MALL

Wow, I bought everything I needed, and I still have money left! I'm going to save it for vacation.

My dad says if we learn good money habits now, we'll use our money wisely when we're older.

101

It is good to earn your own money. You will like[102] the feeling it gives you.

Always do honest work, kids. Avoid taking jobs that are not.

Babysitting is a good way for older kids to earn money.

• wash the car

• rake leaves

• water plants

• mow grass

• shovel snow

• wash dishes

• pull weeds

• wash windows

• take care of pets

Here are some jobs kids can do to earn their own money.

• polish silver

103

The most important thing you can do is learn to **save your money.**

Ask your parents to help you open a savings account.

When you receive money gifts or earn money, deposit it in your account. Then, when you really need some money, you'll have it.

Learn to spend wisely.

- Buy the things you need first. Then, if you have enough money left, buy the things you want.

- Compare prices at a few stores before you buy an expensive item, like a bike.

- THINK before you buy.

Don't make a habit of borrowing or lending money.

That way, it will never cause misunderstandings or bad feelings between you and your family or friends.

A Good Habit

Pledge! Donate! Contribute!
There are so many worthwhile causes.

Give some of what you have to help others.

Rich, poor, or in the middle, you should always be gracious, courteous, generous, and caring.

Become a person who has a rich life, not just a lot of money.

It's not how much money you have, it's what kind of person you are that counts.

109

You can take that to the bank!

CHAPTER TEN
Go For It!

(Do Your Best)

If you're going to take the time to do something, do your best.

Why, Dad?

Because when you do your best, you will be proud of your work. You will feel good. Others will respect you for doing a good job.

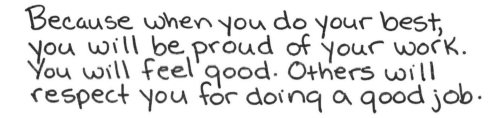

You'll respect yourself, too.

They make it look so easy!

But you know they have worked long and hard to be so good.

ooo That's life, kids.

To be really good at something, you have to practice regularly.

There may be times when you just don't want to practice, but do it anyway.

Train yourself.

Practice makes perfect.

All that practicing will be worth it when you can finally play that difficult song, make a touchdown, get good grades, paint a great picture, or do whatever it is you set out to do.

Doing your best takes time and effort.

But it is worth it!

When you set out to do something, <u>think</u>, <u>use your mind</u>.

Some kids have book smarts- they know a lot of facts.

Some kids have practical smarts- they have a lot of common sense.

Some kids have creative smarts- they express ideas through their art.

It's nice to have all three, it gives you balance, but whatever kind you have...

Use Your Smarts!

When you try something and it doesn't work the first time, don't give up - try, try again.

If it still doesn't work, use your mind, be creative, be imaginative, find another way.

Even when you try your hardest, you're going to make mistakes. Don't give up. Find out what you did wrong, then don't do it again.

Learn from your mistakes.

Most jobs or projects you do have 3 important parts:

1. Get ready (prepare).

2. Do it.

3. Clean up and/or get ready for the next time.

A student writing a report has to:

1. Gather pencil, paper, and notes
2. Write the report
3. Put supplies away and get report ready to hand in

A football player at practice has to:

1. Get out equipment and put it on properly
2. Practice
3. Clean and store equipment so it's ready for the next practice

When there's something you have to do, DO IT!

Don't put it off until the last minute.

Give yourself plenty of time to do a good job.

And remember, when you work with a positive attitude, any job you do will be easier.

Be the best you can be!

One last word about

VALUES...

123

We care about YOU, and we care about the world.

The world needs good people. That's why values are so important

Values help you to know the difference between right and wrong.

We hope the set of values in this book helps you!

IMPORTANT VALUES

Respect Yourself
Use Your Head
Take Responsibility
Get Along with Your Family
Be a Good Friend
Fight Prejudice
Get Involved
Protect the Environment
Use Your Money Wisely
Do Your Best

125

Have a great life, Kids!
Arf-Arf!